My Favorite Guitar Encores

Volume One

by Néstor Ausqui

Grand Concert Flamenca Negra, Ziricote classical guitar by Pimentel Guitars, Albuquerque, New Mexico, USA.

WWW.MELBAY.COM

Prologue

The last note of the printed program floats in the air and a momentary silence lets the sound travel to the most remote corners of the concert hall. The solo guitarist slowly raises his head while his hands leave the instrument. Now the audience, seemingly coming out of a state of ecstasy, begins to applaud and the artist bows and thanks them, then exists the stage without suspending the concentration that the concert program demanded.

The artist returns to the stage to ongoing applause, acknowledging the audience several times until the applause becomes contagious, euphoric, demanding another piece. Now the applause increases and little by little it is transformed into a great random polyphony, "Encore! Encore! Just one more," or "Zugabe! Zugabe!" as they say in Germany. In Spain they demand *propinas* and in many Latin American countries you might hear the popular "Otra! Otra!"

All these expressions used around the world share the same meaning—the concert must be extended! What comes next is not printed in the program and for the concert artist, it is sometimes a challenge to choose an encore piece. Did the concert artist preselect a work to play in this circumstance? Some of them already have favorite works for this purpose, but generally—if the public does not request a specific work—the musician decides **at that moment** which work he or she will play for an encore.

Unlike earlier parts of a concert program, the works in this collection do not require intensive listening. They are neither long nor elaborate. For encores, short familiar pieces that capture the sensitivity of both the musician and the audience, are the best option.

My Favorite Guitar Encores, Volume 1 was conceived as a sensible selection of short works that, throughout the 50 years of Maestro Néstor Ausqui's guitar career, were offered as encores in prominent concert halls in the United States, Canada, and several Latin American and European countries.

No set rules govern which works can be performed as concert encores. The pieces may be slow or fast, secular, or sacred. They can be orchestra or chamber works arranged for a specific instrument. For the guitar, however, works for lute by the masters of the English Renaissance or even the French Baroque period are well suited for this purpose. The works of John Dowland and Francis Cutting provide both the instrumentalist and the audience with characteristic fullness and calm that make them particularly suitable as encores.

Without a doubt, Johann Sebastian Bach should be included in this collection where the complex French style of ornamentation stands out. The guitar arrangement of "Prelude VIII" from *The Well-Tempered Clavier* remains faithful to Bach's writing, again highlighting the French-style ornamentation.

By contrast, "Prelude X" has a different story. It could be said that the Russian composer Alexander Siloti did not arrange "Prelude X" from *The Well-Tempered Clavier*", but rather, "Number 18" from *Das Klavierbüchlein für Wilhelm Friedemann Bach;* Bach himself had already reworked this piece with the goal of creating something that his son Wilhelm could use to learn to play the harpsichord. For his own arrangement, Johann Sebastian used only the first slow part of his original "Prelude X", simplifying the ornamented right-hand part and replacing it with chords.

Siloti used this second version by the senior Bach, "recomposing" it with one simple change to make it more attractive to the post-Romantic tastes of the 20th century. The left hand of the original prelude became the melody, and the right-hand chords became the bass. If Siloti had kept the original key of E minor, it would have meant that the melody would not be in a suitable middle register. That is why Silotti changed the key to B minor; as a result, the melody resides in a medium range and the chords, now in the left hand, provide more intense harmonic support. The guitar arrangement in this edition is based on Siloti's elaboration.

It is well known that the guitar "sings", and its song is as sweet as the human voice. One of Schubert's best-known Lieder, the "Ave Maria", simply had to be included in this encore collection. Naturally, when we hear the Ave Maria, we assume that it was always a religious work. Surprisingly, the original version does not relate to the church but had a secular lyric like any other *Lied; a* young woman implores the Virgin Mary for help with her life and that of her father.

Many pieces in this book have equally interesting backstories that are worth researching and retelling. When your audience demands an encore, may this book serve you well!

Guillermo René Alvarez
Professor of Musicology at the Instituto Superior de Música
Universidad Nacional del Litoral - Argentina

Contents

Captain Digorie Piper's

Arr. and fingering: Néstor Ausqui

John Dowland
(1563-1626)

Guitarra

Arr. Néstor Ausqui

Frog
(Galliard)

John Dowland
(1563-1626)

V.S.

Mr. Knight's Galliard

Arr. Néstor Ausqui

John Dowland
(1563-1626)

Packington's Pound

Arr. Néstor Ausqui

Francis Cutting
(1550-1603)

Guitarra

Preludio VIII

(From “The Well-Tempered Clavier”)

Arr. Néstor Ausqui

J. S. Bach
(1685-1750)

V.S.

23
I
tr
26
I
i m m i a
VIII
A.H.-
II
p
29
a m i
III
32
34
II
VII
36
38
II

Sonata in D minor

(K. 1 L. 366)

Revision and fingering: Néstor Ausqui

Domenico Scarlatti
(1685-1757)

V.S.

19
VIII
V
III
III
21
P m i a m
IV
II
23
III
III
25
27
III
II
III
II
III
II
31

Guitarra

Sonata in A Major

(L. 238)

Arr. and fingering: Néstor Ausqui

Domenico Scarlatti
(1685-1757)

Allegro cantabile

This page has been left blank to avoid an awkward page turn.

Ave Maria

Transc. and fingering: Néstor Ausqui

Franz Schubert
(1797-1828)

La Montfsemell in A minor

(Rondeau)

Guitar

Arr. and fingering: Néstor Ausqui

Robert de Visée
(1655-1725)

33
III
37
III
40

Tombeaux du Vieux Gallot

(Allemande)

Arr. and fingering: Néstor Ausqui

Robert de Visée
(1655-1725)

28
30
34
38
a m i m i m
41
i m i m i i m i m a m i i a m i a i m a
45
m i m
47
1.

Prelude in B minor BWV 855a

(based on a piano version by A. Siloti)

Arr. and fingering: Néstor Ausqui

J. S. Bach
(1685-1750)

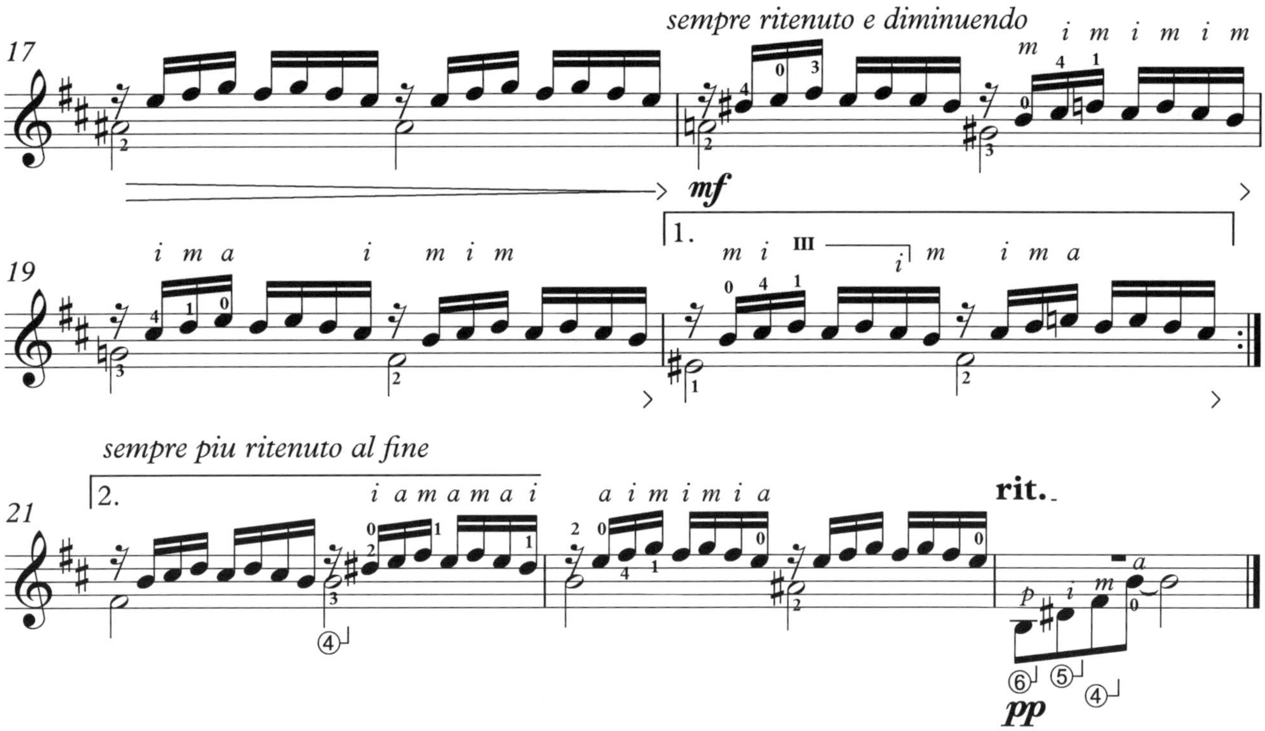
sempre ritenuto e diminuendo
mf
sempre piu ritenuto al fine
rit.
pp

Gnossiennes No. 1

Arr. and fingering: Néstor Ausqui

Erik Satie
(1866-1925)

52
57
63
68
73
78

Danza Eslava Op. 72 No. 2

Guitarra

Arr. and fingering: Néstor Ausqui

Antonín L. Dvořák
(1841-1904)

V.S.

64
72
79
86
92
98
104
110
ar.12
117
122

Adiós a la Guitarra

(elegía)

Guitarra

Néstor Ausqui (revisión y digitación)

Ricardo Almará

46
II
51
56
60
rit.
p

Prelude in E minor

(from *24 Preludes*)

Revision and fingering: Néstor Ausqui

Ricardo Almará
(1975-)

26
cresc.
ff
29
staccato
32
5:4
pp

Angel Dance

(In memoriam of Natalia Rivero Rubianes)

Ricardo Almará
(1975-)

Revision and fingering: Néstor Ausqui

49
53
III
VII
II
56
59
62
65
X

This page has been left blank to avoid an awkward page turn.

Absence

(In memory of Nenuchi)

Revision and fingering: Néstor Ausqui

Ricardo Almará
(1975-)

66
X
VII
72
II
VIII
III
III
VIII
80
I
III
89
III
97
I
III
104
V
VIII
VIII
112
IX
p i m i m

120
129
137
144
151
159
167

172
III
179
184
m a i a i a
190
194
rit.

Luminous Cielo

Dedicated to Mater Dolorosa
Passionist Retreat Center
Sierra Madre California

Revision and fingering: Néstor Ausqui

Cruz Trevino

31
37
IV
II
43
48
53
57

Guitarra

All Quiet Along the Potomac Tonight

(Civil War-Era Song)

Arr. and fingering: Néstor Ausqui

John Hill Hewitt